MW01631279

Made in the USA
Lexington, KY
25 April 2012

LIFE LESSON #21
Don't Pick Your Nose!
Amy Wallace

ISBN: 0-615-29533-9
ISBN-13: 9780615295336
Library of Congress Control Number: 2009903286

In loving memory of my daddy,
George Dawson,
the best Daddy a girl could have.
June 25, 1946-November 25, 2005

To Mama,
you will forever be my rock.

To Micah,
you are the peanut butter to my jelly.

To Sarie,
my gentle one. Without you,
I would not be who I am today.

To Lily,
my free spirit. My inspiration for *Life Lessons*.
Keep marching to the beat of a different drum.

"Let the little children come to me, and do not hinder them, for the kingdom of God belongs to such as these."
Mark 10:14

Use your fingers to pick a flower for your mommy.

But *don't* use
your fingers
to pick your nose!

Use your fingers to pick up your toys.

But *don't*
use your fingers
to pick your nose!

Use your fingers to pet your dog.

But *don't* use your fingers to pick your nose!

Use your fingers to count to ten.

But *don't*
use your fingers
to pick your nose!

Use your fingers
to tie your shoes.

But *don’t*
use your fingers
to pick your nose!

Use your fingers
to draw a picture
of your cat.

But *don't*
use your fingers
to pick your nose!

Boogers and cooties
live in your nose,
and there they
should stay...

...*until* you get a tissue,
blow your nose,
and then
throw them away!

Made in the USA
Lexington, KY
25 April 2012